Dark Would

(the missing person)

Dark Would

(the missing person)

Poems by Liz Waldner

The University of Georgia Press

Athens and London

Published by the University of Georgia Press
Athens, Georgia 30602
© 2002 by Liz Waldner
All rights reserved
Set in 10 on 14 Electra by Bookcomp, Inc.
Printed and bound by McNaughton & Gunn, Inc.
The paper in this book meets the guidelines for
permanence and durability of the Committee on
Production Guidelines for Book Longevity of the
Council on Library Resources.

Printed in the United States of America
06 05 04 03 02 P 5 4 3 2 1

Library of Congress Cataloging-in-Publication Data
Waldner, Liz.
Dark would : (the missing person) : poems / by Liz Waldner.
    p. cm.
ISBN 0-8203-2391-8 (pbk. : alk. paper)
I. Title.
PS3573.A42158 D37 2002
811'.54—dc21   2001008267

British Library Cataloging-in-Publication Data available

Contents

Acknowledgments

"Orpheus Under The Table": *The Boston Review*

"Ho, The Isle Of Lesbos"; "Oars"; "Black Hat Drownded
Piece": *The Columbia Poetry Review*

"Forms of A(d)Dress"; "Bagging It": *Key Satch(el)*

"Memorandum Of Understanding And Plea"; "No Count":
Tinfish

"The Path Leading From Little To Much": *VOLT*

"Exponential Episcopy, If Not Episcopation"; "Dark
Would/To Let/An Era": *Kenning*

"Shrimpy Girl Talk TypoParenthetical": *Outlet/Lucy House*
chapbook and website

"Diptych: Portrait Of Self As St. Anthony . . .": *LIT*

"Reins, Annals": *Jubilat*

"A History Of Dust"; "Projector: A Lover's Lament"; "Twin
Hymns": *Antennae*

"A History Of Divinity": *The Colorado Review*

"A History Of Dust"; "A History Of Divinity"; "The Shrimpy
Girl Talk"; "Attendance"; and "Noah Takes Five" are
included in *CALL*, a Meow Press chapbook, 2000.

Thanks to VCCA and Djerassi, where much of this was written.

A thing is always a this one.
HEIDEGGER, *What Is a Thing?*

Mid-way this life's journey, I came to myself in a dark wood . . .
DANTE, *Purgatorio*

Lucus a non lucendo.

Where There's A Will (Away)

The stone lion's head is dank. No
fault of its own: its bushes want
trimming. Here the desire
to read *Alice* whose hair
wanted cutting arises as desire
does: oblique, out of something else.
Here is one such: the bird alights
atop a flowery stem of rosemary AND

(I quote) *the walls do not fall.*
My flowers, my walls—

Did you really think I'd say?
"The stone lion" (I'll say)
has wings of stone: it can
think but not make *away.*

Only *write* avails.
To leaf. To leave.
To flee. To fleece.
Be stone(d): write:

My hair wants cutting. I'll—
stay—
say—
do it today.

i.

Various Ways of Questioning about the Thing

. . . for example, a prayer is a logos but neither true nor false.

ARISTOTLE, *On Interpretation*

A/ppeal A/pple A/dam A/dream

It was too hot. I put the fan in the window and me in the bed
And the linen sheet only to cover my ribs.

When I woke, I heard some bird had turned the sky
To water in its probably lavender throat.

I'd dreamed I'd had a hose and walked, watering
A lawn.

Some had come to me for the water I was.
One I never saw went with me watering the lawn.

Next, you sent me a letter: sorry it's been so long
But I'm moving the buttons on the coat I bought you.

A strange shape of cloth like a blue tomato carefully pinned
In a gray tissue came with it. What is it?

I unpinned pins until I saw the wrapper bore pictures of pins
In the places they'd been.

When I put them back in, I woke. When I woke I wore that coat
You knew how to fit instead of my skin.

Friend, come button me in.

Washed Clean By The Blood

I could correlate
    each of these bird calls
to the thought
    you do not call

to the thought
    one thing indicates
an other. What if
    (the other's purview)

every time I think of you
    you think of me
and I don't know it.
    Plenty not to know

I note. I think of you
    all the day and in the night
and they are long. I long
    to believe most
of my thoughts are wrong.

Listen carefully.
    Bird song.
I would make come of it
    some good Thing.
Without much charity

was nothing made all
    along.

Being And Seeming, In Public

i.

I sit by a little glop of bird poop
and a cough walks by.
"A likeable young breeze"
is in the recommended trees.

"Don't think too long
how should we live knowing
that we must die,"
the leaf sound hurries by.

Sun gleams on my keychain.
A plastic bag rustler observes the sky.
A red notebook holder in German shoes
smiles a bespectacled "Hi."

She's in on this though gone,
another leaf written on,
another page blown by.

ii.

Nobody likes to walk in front of you sitting on a bench watching
them walk by. This I deduce from faces going by. I'd thought
I was alone in this. I'm alone on the bench. But kindly, I sport
alarming yellow droopy beaded earrings as potential diversion:
here, look at these and don't feel so inspected, alone, on display!
But instead he lit a cigarette to manage the return passage. A
thing to be busy with, what walkers in front of bench-sitters

need. Like push your glasses up your nose, one of my ploys. Oh, having a visible body, variable difficulties, variable joys.

My little flappy sunglasses attachments are on cock-eyed, I re-alize. Maybe I'm alone in this, after all; maybe it's for thinking I'm nuts they avert their eyes.

iii.

O O O, walking around in my flippy new sundress, I'm in drag. I've shaved a whole lot of leg, though a few wooly portions may still reveal themselves high on my thighs as my skirt flip flips. Hello I'm in disguise as a girl, I have on a bra, a thing not donned since junior high and you don't know it's weird, you I don't know think it's me! O strange and untoward to finally look normal to others (could it be?) by finally being completely beyond the pale—invisible—to me.

iv.

Here they give you the shadow of your hand.
Here they give you the shadow of your hair.
Here are people passing on a tour.
The shadow of a stem of grass forks just here.

Here is how to mend the passed:
hear wind move trees like this.
Add courtyard, sun, and dry
to the How Should We Live list.

Forms Of A(d)Dress

Hello, lizards. I am back, although dressed in the wrong skin.

The shadow of a wheelbarrow pulls the shadow of a smaller man.

Than you are, large of hand and with your skin so generous. There is welcome rain and there is flood. There is welcome sun and there is parch. All, at once. Parchman, the farm whose rows have ever hard to hoe been. Labor, deliver herself. Others, from evil. Primeval, prime rate, borrow nickel, dime, quarter; time free for all, yet scarce, high-priced: we bought weeks with the rest of our lives.

When the boss lady walked by holding up her plastic-bagged evening wear like the hand of a man in a minuet, like a fish on the line, I was feeling the filament of particularly fine long blond hair that makes its home not far from my wrist. I'd say I was feeling in a speculative way, and pulling a little, a shadow, too; trying a lizard's skin. I heard her heels hollow, quick on the walk and looked and saw but didn't see if she'd seen me dreamily fingering, how embarrassing.

What if everything were named for what you do with it or what it does with you. Walk on walk. Dream on dream. Row on row. These trees mountain mountain. I've seen a cloud cloud and I've seen a cloud mountain. I cannot say you mountain me but like a fountain limber music in. Thinking on this, thinking on this thinking, I cannot say a thing.

Deliverance

Skin like a lizard, shaped like the head
of a lizard, these leaves like a lizard
(something) the sun.

Tongue, swallow, fatten, feed; are made, done
up over in by for with to: the historical prepositional
litany, its last moment in the sun.

O Rusty the lover and rusty the state
fallen from me now like the skin of my heel
I left on the gate.

O to have such a message addressed especially to me
of words un-underpinned by prelate's guilt
a restless shade named Atone . . .

O to have again your little note: "I smell you
on me and surely love." Here I am alone.

(Come on, words, don't be shy,
cri de coeur is fine.)

Only the dead leaf moves, curled brown
dry light, turns in the least wind
on an I guess invisible thread

for I guess something there is holds me too
ear to the ground of a one who never
makes the sound COME

I stay like a lizard where no sun is, desire
shaped like a faith in words' faithlessness;
"Out of love," for instance

turns both ways and might as well mean
something else will again
with something else spell "love" . . .

Primer

whose spirit is this, we asked . . .

cimarron. durango. alamosa. How Green Was My. lie laylain.
in state. *outcast state.* (understate). not in vain. my name, my
other name. my mouth, my other mouth. its speech all day.
show forth. *deaf heaven.* thy praise.

pool. pray: chant the names of the vulva all day. *concha, paloma.*
all day food in, language out. same mouth. sweet mouth. slip. go
south. lip it lightly. sip, sip, *where sucks the bee, there suck I.* speak
to me not only. with. at, to, for. breath body breath in, O *brave
new world* out. *words of the fragrant portals.* doubled *artificer,
measure to me* my solitude. the sound of my name, Without.

. . . because we knew it was the spirit that we sought.

"Eros and Philos, we'll alternate." *We'll be God's spies.* current
state; sweet s(w)immer. clouds up over the water for tea. clouds
like slow fish swim up over the mountains, the shape of your
shoulders arced over me. the shape of the body I will no longer
see. the weight of your left breath swims a shadow through my
belly, turns in my blood long after what casts it ("with silken
line and silver hook") is gone from me. fishes for me. hook tears
a way in my mouth for a story:

borning forty years then love comes to deliver. grow new skin.
hymen. fore- at. to: with every letter—god as your word
twisted into me, cochlea, concha, inland sea—waves weave up
w/hole a wounded speech to heal by being broken anew.

now let me break.
        and not   yet.
              first make the sun still, and the moon,
and this weather. make every longinged Before a credit in love's
ledger. or undo number; make leaves of the wings of the calen-
dar: evergreen, let them stay, these days. or make going go away.
or as a yearned wave into your inner ear, let me go, and gone, stay.

like a body wholly body, fluttering its empty sleeves.

make me not afraid of Empty.
not of Unmade.

Interpretation

Why sorry? Because unreached for
because the one who,

to be reachable, must not
reach (for) me.

Not even true.
Reached and then some.

Only a certain kind of flower
for a certain kind of bee.

Here's one favors rosemary;
I favor impossibility

and the fragrance of might
but couldn't be.

I am sick of being
this bee.

I.D.

The view out the window is
dead mouse. Belly up.

White belly, a patch
like the skins of sunlit grass
or shadow's debate on the bark
of that tree: be, not be.
Have you left
your wife? Have you left
for me? What's left
(for) you? "The world
has shown me so little mercy,"
you cried. This world,
all-merciful, also
has shown you an idea
with a relative inside:

window. Probably there
is nothing else to see.

Looks Are Everything

It turns out there is a large white rectangle with a tall white cylinder on top of the knob of the long blue ridge of low mountain I call my view. Out of adjectives for the day. Two branches of some shrubby tree reach up like calipers or crab claws to frame it at the back of the near field. "Field" came out "filed" when I first typed it; everything filed according to how it seems to me. Can't there be another way? Do I ask out of pain? The same aeiou's as pleasure, and also as endlessly elaboratable as breath. As if vowels knew the name of god, their hiding itself the sound of this name.

What? I mean, two shot stalks of wild asparagus lie prone on their tentacles where a more meager but upright third stands guard. I mean, who watches over us when we fall over with the elaborately named bloom of our disbeliefs? I am tired, you say, and it turns out this is not a shattered tea bowl and not like death. A morning moment's grayness came out full mourning dress. Came out shards, misnamed, a weak tea of distress.

I mean, it turns out you and I who make a bowl in the morning are not a bowl at the end of the day. I don't know where you are, you say, but I don't go away. Which language reflects this change of state in its names? Something Pueblo, who made their houses out of clay. Because what looks lost isn't ever far away, because tomorrow is now as is yesterday?

What we found, lost. Foundation. Where is our house hiding? Aspects imperfectible, always out in the storm of *o dokei moi* like Lear but lost without a Fool. To walk *as if*. Last night the haze hid the house on the hill, but the tree branches held its place. Like wings.

Like wings made of leaves at the garden's gate. The wings made of leaves, the gate made of wings. Wing and gate look the same from the garden. Let day speak to day with the tongues of leaves and night to night with the tongues of day. If "if", if likeness is all that I can have, I'll call its field belief to have the look of a place to live with you. Let it call me into what I can't see but might find in the field of my body. My name contains a house within it. Look at, look for, me that way.

Reins, Annals

i.

There is a field. The last light falls on a field
and so it becomes the field of light. The field of light
drains as the sun drops to the mountaintop.
This is steepletop. Then was rain.

ii.

The pale nakedness of the birch,
I name it with the wanting of a body.
But first I knew it was beautiful,
or so it occurs to me to say.

iii.

In the afternoon, annular, the cloud
siphoned to earth by the alphabet of birch.
Multitudes of milk-white rivulets
channel shape-shifting drift,
in deft and elemental conversion
and, as with Tree in general,
a profound and utter
poise and fervor.

Say: prepare, for the light kingdom comes.
Pray: press your face to the tree's bright sex.
Send your white words up
through the channels of whiteness
running down the glass
of the great cow sky.

O Suzanna

Spindle. Dirndl. Ice cream bathing
Beauty on a stick. The needle's prick.

Snow white and so
Back to cream, ice & cold.

Bathing could be read as loathing
In hand-writing bad as mine. Why

Bother? The briar-eyed-out lover's
Already in a lather. The Bawth Motif.

(Bath mat, breasts and Baden Baden
Beat the hastiest retreat . . .)

Noah Takes Five

Paloma—to make a breath.
Beheld, I felt.

P is not a nice sound
but I want my spine
pressed deep in the dirt
at the sound of your name.

Dirt, where are you now?
(Only the spirit of things has a name).

What can I do?
(She rose).

The eyes between my fingers close.
The eyes between my legs she won't.
(The unknown through the more unknown).
Shall I shout on the phone?

There's a button for numbers.
The button for flower's a hole.

No desire for a thing unknown.
I want the little leaf.
I want the little dove.
I want the epithalamion flower.

—But O Father William,
you are old . . .

Memorandum Of Understanding And Plea

Mime new tennis shoes, bony knees;
sing *rough weather, plural water,*
The Rhyme Of The Ancient Mariner;
engage in the production of signs.
Let this be an act of faith.

Say "daddy, big and grand
are all co-terminus; size
and distance are not understood
in any absolute sense."
Let this be an expression of desire.

A measured silence, then to cry—
though time is not meant to be exhaustive,
let me hear her say again
"Thank you for being so interesting
in so short a period of time."

The Model

You say you think she likes you
The parking lot attendant, too
"Many things thought of doing to her" said

Penny Lane hummed in sun
follows Under My Thumb:
"Siamese CAT of a girl"—for sure

To have things done to one
What one wishes after all
Hair done, done up, done wrong

"ooh she done me, she done me good"
She done some dishes after sex and food
But not all, not all . . .

The need for sunglasses an interruption
Go and get them. *Go and catch a falling star* . . .
It's late July, the other coast . . . *all past years are* . . .

I'm done. Done for. Far gone. Unfair:
Our days there an obsolete model
In perfectly good repair.

Gretel *Insomne & Insondable*[1]

Morpheus[2] followed her logic so far—
her lodgings, their hangings & other Expects—
then left for the View From Above.
Opera glasses were all his rage; hers was
(You see? he'd say) in effect Left.

Hers left. *gules droit.*[3] Only (Or-
ly[4]—she's never been, gone, done—*on
fait*, -fe?[5]) a tracing remained, an
archipelago of saltish stain, sol
long (*ma langue*[6]) so (lo)ng(e)[7].

At night there are leaves (so many leaves),
she sees. Pelagic, a sea on the moon,
she says. And descries:
beneath to bequeath is belief . . .
bereft. Nonetheless.

---

1. Gretel, Sleepless & Deep.
2. god of sleep; double for Orpheus (and *Orfée*, hence the upcoming opera glasses, and view)
3. heraldry; part of a heraldic device. gules: color red. droit: Fr. right
4. Orly, suburb of Paris—and its airport. ly-on: lion (heraldic reprise. red lion of the Rider Tarot deck)
5. on fait: Fr. one does, is done. fe: Sp. faith: take it on faith, this particular opera began in Santa Fe . . .
6. Fr. my language, my tongue
7. Fr. songe, dream

Diptych: Portrait Of Self As Saint Anthony With Visitation By Saint Jerome

Did Bosch do me? He ought (Why not?
What's "dead"? "Ought to" or "ought
to have done"—*son* one.): bedeviled
by a bevy of pesky noises,
I can't stand my skin; the sound burns in.
The wind wounds. Gangrenous
grotesqueries, ergonometries
of nerve over-worked (ergotism the ego
caught with a case of the id's bends:
I kink, *ergo* I am . . .): *Ay*, I, fiery sands . . .

Pobrecito, San Anton (a pigeon shat
in your public square, a fillip that
lit in my fiery hair, mortifying solitaire):
everywhere, not just the hands,
a filigree of paper-cuts—filet *de mí*—sol, re, *tí*

do me. He-she, hand in the small of my back
as I passed before and through the door
is a sudden silence hours after. A hieroglyph,
I muse, and in me sings the Lennon tune:
"She done me, he done me good."
Do you, too, goddesses who
watch over women in deserts; deliver from rack
and ruin once again your humble devotee of IF.

    Hieronymous, hierogrammat (she prays),
    Show forth thy ciphers as thy praise,
    hier and *if* the laboring slaves

now-and-then, the hinge between
old torment and "(some) new pleasure."
Into my days, write full measure.
Manuscript, manumit, scribe my skin
From without as within. Write "me"
with touch. "The book is enough."

Who was the saint that was flayed?
The lion girl is back again.
I saw her on the Madrid train.
Exquisite. She wants,
(I wish) she says, (what else
is new beneath this insistent sun
in this Spanish Little Egypt?)
a she to _____ and to have done
her good. Me (the verb), I would
("to jane," q.v.).
May be.
Let's say (quietly)
Es por eso "e-special" pain
she has stayed
and stays.

Ho, The Isle Of Lesbos

Tolle legit!

AUGUSTINE'S *Confessions*

The distinction between men and women
is an important matter to the state.
I have feelings for you, as the inarticulate
say. SweetBee says: Go fish.

Like Alice, I am a-swim. A fish is
a secret sign for a secret meeting:
dear sexy thing, meet me @ the catacombs
with goldfish crackersnacks. A whim,

apoplectic poetics: 7-ish and Richter
scales fell away from my eyes.

In tears. Stella Maris, world wide
kitchen faucet drip, the tides.
Who can ignore them? *Dear efforts at being*
in the sinks of our lives . . .

I sniff when you say "androgynous,"
you so-and-so with lace on your socks.
In Moby Dick, the whale's penis
is worn for a cassock:

Is "Take up and eat!" an unholy page
from a Great White Book?

The Nonne Priest's Tale

i. *Absence (Aprille Shoures)*

He said "dirts"; this made me love him,
also smile over a pot of hot water sixteen years
later again in a kitchen not mine.

If I say it right (Lust suggests with its own reasons)
he'll come out of the rain and we'll head for my bed
again and undo it for sixteen years.

ii. *Semi-Presents (Epicene)*

I want to pick her penis
a little like a flower
and plant it carefully.
Bloom in me, muse;
indeed, your thighs are worthy
of dozens of sighs and scribes.
He looks to be all tomboy bones;
I want to make his eyes roll
and his ribs groan with pleasure.
This rough power—
no bones about it—
does not in the green fuse lie.

iii. *Outward And Visible Form*

The woman I rent from in Massachusetts
suspects I barf after meals.
(She's jealous and fat, my friend opines.)

Pitching a look at her husband, she cries,
You're so skinny! and comes over to feel.
I am, rather, sexy but here ignore it:
it's a car door open to offer a ride,
trouble when you travel alone. Outside
the South, you can hardly afford
to walk, nevermind ride. O cold snide
Boston, I'm in the poor house, now.
Alas for the bone house,
I remember her well—
enough to counter in any kitchen:
What's skinny got to do with skin?
Taste and see—on credit.

Dr. Denouement

the mended cloud   the evening tree

    dark footprints through the dew

the silent bird   the empty egg

    signs only she can read

crows ate the right way home   knuckles   jam
    crumbs on a plate   iris and lily
too Burne-Jones for her taste

on her knees she licks the dew
    to trace a print to make her have gone
where she wanted her to

                a sign

someone—

late, alone
had come: (to mean)

    I was desired
    (ever prayer)

        door   ajar

that shape of reach
that moment hope

                    to open the story
                         the mother story

the stamen   golden   story

but
pollen, brass
        a little burning
and then
it's only flies

Self Portrait As Platter On Wall

Shadow puppet heads embossed in brass.
Who makes my thoughts go always to you?
I tried sawing through my neck to look
fixed like these, to sever be from do, to

as those with throats intact could say, no avail.

Here is where I who've never had trouble with No
cannot say No. My own Salome.
If only I cared to dance jubilantly
about a Pyrrhic victory. Seven veils

as tourniquet and still I bleed. Unfortunate.

In Chinese astrology, my birth date makes me
a metal monkey. "Rough on words," indeed.
Bronze, steel. Take my head, refreshing foundry.
Impress, anneal. Take my head and change my mind.

Shrimpy Girl Talk TypoParenthetical)

the plastic bag is urgent in the breeze:
fog is coming over the ridge
cat is sleeping in the planter

i listen but that's all

o bad girl, bad shrimpy girl
she eats the forbidden fruit, she
says gossip, she wants her hours back,
she pours bad beer in the potted plant, she
wishes not any more, Boston is
good for her, ugly and mean and full
of things to hurt about with a pen, no
wonder she can't hear what's—

good lord a flly is boxing with white gloves on the black ground
of a photagrapsh. not a fily, but a fly. filly. yesterday I carried
horsehair in a bag by some horses with blue hoods over their
eyes. the eye slits were sewn shut with white thread. remember
the shrunken head in the cleveland museum. natural history,
sold butterflies, too. it's too easy to yell about SELLS. the fly has
eaten its boxing gloves or boxed them off while I wasn't looking.
how largely good not to be in control, I almost finished writing
when I heard the neighbor coughing up phlegm in the bath.
shrimpy girl may ever fault herself, she so fears faulting. and
amazingly today the day is cool.

photagrapsh. grasps the moment, grabs the bargain from the
bargain bin. (look, what a life, let's buy it) the voice of droll is

heard in the land. the 17 year locusts fall down to sleep again for 17 years. how do they hear their own song?

barn swallows barnstorm, roll blue feathers through the air, carom, describe the swell of cumulus and never get it wrong. thunder, also, never wrong. "The bruised blue of wrong."

A bit of moss caught in the fence, messy where the grid is strong and only definition, longs. The breeze reveals its longing. That's my own breath—the barn swallows up like two dozen teacups tossed on a blanket—flight's hushing song and noise of prayer. How does it go? Noise is like nuts in French; hence Bedlam as a name that spread, that left, that leaves. I think it's *l* but it's *s*. I think it isn't but it is—ok. Sieve, sieve, sieves.

The plastic bag rattles on; now the newspapers respond. They'll tell me if it's urgent. (I doubt, therefore I am. Me. Tarzan, and also Jane. How could I have failed to hear the names. Shrimpy Girl is doubly bad, so really very good.

What's urgent is my need to say, Ecce, where's the girls?

Portrait Of Self As Potted Plant

Bless'd beyond compare
except potted.

The Shrimpy Girl Talk

El Camarón is a red hook on a yellow card in the game of *Lotería.*

For the last three months, I bought my broccoli in the town of
Red Hook in Dutchess County, NY, although the broccoli did
not grow in the ground of Red Hook.

It is hard to say if I grew in or near the ground of Red Hook; if
I became accomplished or grew fatigued or waxed enthusiastic
as some vegetables are waxed—

which fact, in fact, enables me to state with conviction I did not
wax enthusiastic, did not wax anything at all in comparison—yet

I recall those inexplicable outrages, power outages, outlandish
accesses of unjustifiable annoyance with the one I lived with in
the stone tower near the village of Red Hook, the stone abode
featured in the poem "The Ballad Of Barding Gaol," if you'd
like to know and right now I am unexpectedly in the midst of
one of those angry annoyances and departing on its way from
my prepared text:

it is annoying to try to work with refrigerators and voices like
fire engines and here a cigarette and there a newspaper observa-
tion; on the other hand, the assigned work room has only a tiny
table parked in front of a sliding door, and the computer screen
back lit ruins the eyes as quickly as the table underneath which
my legs don't fit unless I lower the chair so that the computer
is at my chin and my hands reach up to pray ruins my wrists

well but girls know no one will like them if they say so and I have said so only to find the saying and not are like the stone tower and so back to our scheduled program, the stone abode near the village of Red Hook, this one Dutch, not Spanish

though neither are in evidence, were, I mean for I am no longer there, I am here, though soon I will not be and already four days of CA cars and wantonly awful children and a two-hour tale of woe aimed at my ear, no my heart, no, I dunno at what but I trembled

as does the little sea in the inner ear, disturbed by the sounds from the mouth that said and said what never assembled itself into story and for that reason was traffic, more, the glare and misery of horribles we spread on arteries like cholesterol throughout what was this green and pleasant land

but forgive me, I preach, who once upon a time testified at tent revival meetings and spoke most humble, the truth and spoke in tongues which never smell of didact or speak of precept and are, indeed, pure percept, the holy ghost's feeling on a morning full of fog when it wakes in its room too small and dark to write in to discover its desk lamp doesn't work after it had to take a sleeping pill and isn't

no, I don't. eat shit.

such outages and accesses are a species of wax, specie, a dreadful word, how good all over america children are not learning to say feces but poo poo, bm, #2. how brilliant is #2, or even as I laughed uproariously, capitol L, capitol U (the name of an odd, tubular kind of cookie one can encounter on the shelves of grocery stores in places one doesn't particularly like—capitol with an o or an a? an omega or an alpha? how near am I to either?) to discover that a childhood playmate's family called it pieces, a discovery that has informed my appreciation of life itself, a thing that must be obvious, a thing I am not at all sure I want to have said or is true and after all, in my family (if you can call it that) (and who are you, I might as well ask, again) we called it—dare I speak its name?

not red hooks, I hasten regretfully to inform; it is never my intent to misinform as they, journalists or politicians, whoever, say: Miss Inform, she wears a sash, a crown, high heels, a Slim Line bathing suit—as if Adam could have mistaken his rib for a snake s they passed before him, all the aminals, and he settled the crown of their names upon them singly, each, to be known, a rigor and a pleasure at once—and yet

to take, to mis-take. to take form, take in, dust, a rib, ay, there's the rub, slings, arrows, and all fall down, perchance to wake, down a-down . . .

I see the dreaded word "posy" on the horizon, the fault of the Elizabethans, easy to say as I sit here named Elizabeth on an earthquake fault beneath Bear Gulch Road, although I never say my name is Elizabeth, the beth of which means house, a thing I never have, and Eliza and Elisha mushing their consonants in service toward God who sings this tune: "Doe a dear, a female deer; Jane a servant in my house; me a game I call myself—" The part about how far God is, I will not repeat for it is a kind of fault, though on whose part bears scrutiny, I think

never my intent, yet scrutiny does pare, and to 'gloss over' may be said to have been waxed; *personal emotional hygiene*, as the awful She said, and line cookery; the knife makes *between* and surely there are too many already, lines, cuts, bleeds, waxes as

it shines, lunar calendar, thirteen, the shiny number, mind, an-
other numb-er and also mind, the knife. Between that of its
names and this, El Camaron is a red hook. Hang it on the tides,
the moon that makes them, the hand that feels them, inside,
out; the mouth, its darkness, tongue and teeth through which
pass, have passed, horseradish in cocktail sauce in New Orleans
where a little head and chest rolled on a board through the
sewage-y street

and the city's wet heat, French not Dutch but with some buried
Spanish treasure, the idea of blood good as gold, drawn into
quarters, an Octoroon, a whore of surpassing worth, her ancestry
given in pieces of eight by a hand draped in Brussels lace at rest
on pantaloons among the banana fronds of the French Quarter,
the c(o)unt of counts as black and white counters are placed
by the board; your tricks cost less, pay more if you're dealt a
crazy eight, the sign of infinity squeezed in the middle on its
way through our cells . . .

Eight. Octagon, the shape of the plantation house. Blue moon,
Spanish moss, blue room, the state of mind, the room of state,
the uterine ship of fools, the first floating casino docked at Port
Fate, *les jeux sont faites*, your hand dealt, delta, the river's, delta,
the fourth letter, bodied forth, half of eight, the egg's imperfect
circle, the one, and take-it-away leaves three, triune, Neptune,
the three-in-one present in th(r)ee card draw, draw means tie,
a rope to a red hook, a rope twined of the fibers that make the
laid bond, post bond, mail, beloved, bail another thing to do
with hooks and ships and the hanging of ropes

fibers, a cloth with a fine hand, Clotho the name of one of the
Fates who tailors a suit of cards for you while destiny waits in
the shape of you cut, fit, to be tied with the thread of your

thought, the thread of your story, the threads of all whose lives you've twined

to a red hook on a yellow ground in the game of *Lotería*.

Climb your whole life up your life.

ii.

The Thing as the Bearer of Properties

> . . . would gladly have that which they love be the truth.
>
> ST. AUGUSTINE, *Confessions*

Automat

Why should I eat a peach?
There's a mountain to climb
lungs to burn, other legs to beat
up to the top of the sky at night

Lie in the road for starts, for stars—
it's all too high key

for me, something more sullen, please:
the grated knee, the intimacy
come of a certain suppliancy
due to the skin of the mountain taken

away yet proper to the orbit
of the girl, *Why Pear?*

Not to choose is all—
is every Thing (in thrall)

Grape Nuts

Now I'm hungry.
Now the shadows of the needles
lacerate the trunks of trees.
Hmm, do I hurt?
I'm trained to be
intransitive.

Note only how lovely
against washed-silk, purple-shirted me
the orange of a carrot stub
at rest in the bowl of the stainless spoon
at rest in the bowl of cantaloupe
like a catapult loaded up and ready to throw
Ouch as a message from don't-scream

me. Anyway, I wouldn't scream, I'd moan.
Learned this from a dream; I woke
to find the terrible sound was me.
All those offerings—
needles in veins, dicks in mouths—
wasted on closing
the mouths of the god.
They're only open encouraging
me to finish off

me. What's better for breakfast?
The skin of a mountain?
All of the bra(i)n, none of the mess,
nobody else's cup of tea.

Another Ghost And Where She Came From (stage(f)right)

i.

The ghost girl's fog
at the window again.
Does she want
some porridge?

A candle in its holder
is held. Behold—

But no. Your hand
is not allowed,
blow it
out.

Make a wish
of your touch
on the ghost girl. Make
a wish on the ghost girl's want.

So the ghost girl's wish is the smoke you blow?
No, the ghost girl wishes for skin.

The skin of a mountain?
The ghost of a cloud. A billow of curtain, burn.
Make the ghost girl cry

out,
      loud

ii.

    sat in the back breathing lily of the valley
    saw 2 bugs copulate up in a cloud
    heard a plane exhale, exciting the holly
    the mouths of the flower to the skin of my mouth

    there for a change and held
    and how

iii.

    allowed
        as how I left

    my body
    to leave
        this wanting

        my body
    to all that is
        left of aloud

Role-Call

Come in, flies
and sound of flushing toilets, please come in.

The habit of invisibility weighs heavy today.
Undress, what's life?
a bone? a whisper?
light cream? a clench?
An empty place at the table set
when they've already eaten
and all gone away.

Ghost's opposite?
Absence of a shadow.

I'm all shadow.
Bird song bleeds out of me as substance
therefore. I go
away.

Mere shade of monthly blood
wash the way toward egglessness.
The golden one, the one egg-script
to keep . . .

Call me greedy ovary,
reluctant volcano.
I wear the skin of a mountain,
pretend obliviousness to noise;

that's how you may know it's me today:
such tolerance an obvious disguise.

A Particularly Holey Ghost

Ob der wohl kommt, wenn man ruft?
RILKE, *"The Idiot's Song"*

What words are going to let it out?
"Black matter" and "meaty flies"
aren't mine.

Make it be: The party and nobody
came worth something;
the universal

hope dashed up against the rock and what's
the rock-es name? It's
"All The Same."

Dear Sexual Nemesis,
put it in your pocket then
hold up your empty palm and ask,

What on earth is this?

Alone with the Alone, like Guadalajara,
won't do. What's the point of no
one knows it's you?

What's the point
of calling a rock a simple tune,
hoping to catch on, get carried away when

you'll only come back to haunt yourself one day,
then able to say, "Oh yeah—"
and sing along?

What's the point of Long Long Long and yearn and
Name That Tomb? The rock is all
that's left of you.

Me, who are you?
Why don't you come when I—
Yes, yes, Rilke, it's a nice red ball . . .

MoreSkin

i. *The Annunciation*

there's an empty
bed all night

ii. *Its Memoried Processional*

then went:
Here Come
The Warm Jets
walking the hot wet
album under arm dark
to the boy door
house—knock, enter—needle seek till he comes and go:
this was fine by me,
I knew the way

but now: want

to scream to shake (perchance to dream)
the head back, the head forth
addressing one who surely won't
ever be un(ad)dressed:
what do you?
want from me?

want from me
like at a letter's
end: love,
(some urgent Girl)

and then? not—why not?—any/different,
it's the same as it ever was
before an empty
bed

iii. *Its Self-Addressed Anvil Hope*

deer girl, don't blow (Job, see above)
the whistle, someone will know
your want: out

yet

the skin of a mountain looks easy
easy
easy
to tear

O might O night my blood
be anonymous
enough

O dear—

I'm the wrong I
there are mountains
and there are mountains in the way

but someone might be you—
night be—

enough

in the meantime

continue more and
more to—

hope sheets
without stain
are all night skin for
there's an empty
bed all right

Dark Would/To Let/An Era

and Being, but an Ear
DICKINSON

idea of enough paltry.
hear's an anger.
"O and a gash"—well

enough alone;

rent me a little
space
in your body make
me a loan

with thee

Alone ("lo, in the middle of the wood
the folded leaf from out the bud is woo'd.")
there's an idea.
do it,

(a)lo(ne),

to me
or let (et cetera)
[aria]

my spine reed
time's vowels alone.

Os / Tensorium

i.

colors swim
called refraction
skim *fraktur*
shin, the bone of teeth

possible skin:
"is human what we really mean?"
the snaky 'O' of light
the os

opening to//the #3
resulting
aurora: Might Have Been: aural
smell of the sea

melody of
in-me
this note, that road
pain ("I wd have it again")

why stick at 3?
8?
skin heel on gate
keeper a name

for The Perfect Thing
body so kept

can't finger slide
my little into your dark

thigh where I lick
what daylight does
a kitten's caul
of sleep

what bitter cup?
a brush of leaf
mustache antique
the curlew waking

divide "up"

ii.

gravity's difficult refrain:
        refrain.

iii.

down the drain is not how to feel
to be kind to be wise to be generous.
to be good and clean as a cube of ice—
missed class for dishes that day.

meltwater. front range. where to go.
dayhike. pack animal. measured snow.

a sight to swell you at a distance
shrink you once inside when what
is wanted is—

I forget . . .
the door opened wide?
by other hands, othered.
by other hands, my-ed.

I on my side
("ma in her kerchief and I in my—")
presenting bones
to spine.

throne to dogs.
penetrate: hide.

fat animal
mother of language
say: come. live. inside.

A History Of Dust

Palfrey rode (her pickup truck): dry.
Swallow them up as Moses' rod: miles.

That milk-white one, that wrought-one heed;
Not monstrous but miraculous—and silencing.

Indeed, inbred conspiracy, foil of fashion,
Some of the women so exactly—

A thunderbolt (instead of a squib) in tender toil,
Bodies terrestrial entirely unable

To fib. Grasping a Globe, glib, by all hailed,
The figures which stand by her bed now reviled.

Upon my mind, tired, be gainsaid.
Territory and trial—may pardon prevail.

Do what thou wilt. Whoever how
Doubted his courage. "In infancy."

—In dollars alone, did I say?
She lives upon grasshoppers (not fancily)

After the manner of the dew.
Its double in falling, she has no

Home to go to. Go to. Shoe leather. Rough weather.
Nor ear hath heard, "Come hither, come hither."

However, black and white the license plate ahead
On the Old Dominion road read:

EAT FTHR. Assail, back. So beguiled
Yet naught availed . . .

A History Of Divinity

What did I do one day?
I tried to be loved.

I have still the mask I used.
Are you very pleased about it?

Yes, let us stay here.

*

But the button has come off!
Out of the reach of hope.

Oh! nameless homeless (no one)—
No one in particular?

Why then, I must be blameless.

*

Let's see, could not be
Gain said that I have lain

In a creek, in a car, in a pine-needled ditch
On the side of the road at night—

Personification of the Logos?
Truth of flesh—

(sweet receiv'd, believèd sweet)

And fucked.
No one in particular?

Swallowed them up as Moses' rod
And wept an Exile's amputations.

"To speak with such enthusiasm
Ends in Revelations."

Projector: A Lover's Lament

Imagine what conjectures
this good creature's

teeter-totter bird call
must conclude and limit all

minor third scarce believes
I may redeem a lost year's love

possessive every one and thing
would suffer not the late bird's song

err impatient of control
—know, nor desire to know

sweet, sweet the cry last night
cross dresses left, disguises right;

poses *haute*
proves a kite

to check. body. blow. ye winds
a mind to break my heart sends

an agent of the Pretender sooner
my undoer than my mender—

volatile spur to my resolution
ends in doorless desolation

Twin Hymns

i. *The Truth Out(s)doors*

> 2 shades of green
> > happiness (one would hope)
> a minute long:

> slivery bugs
> > into each other plugged
> upon a black lunch box

> open on a black day:
> > s/he cannot love me
> (despite what s/he say)

ii. *Gotten With The Program Sore*

> One detains by touching
> Too? Was it ever so?

> With brief deliberation
> Been used to make excuses

> Prepared for another world's uses
> The which no longer—bereft—obtains.

> All my woe washed into it
> Others profitably Serious

> (books read, comment made
> annotations Pain's)

My heart beneath it trawls for y'all's
Inquires, Whether . . . ? Tolls—put paid.

For nothing was more—
How now, are you crept hither?

—to me than thee
I left.

Oars

Myth, there I'll begin:
from a sea cliff leap unmanned men

No help for the tied in me
for in hand

I've *brother*, an idea
oaken, graven—*he* . . .

Salt eaten, sky fell, his bone hull
painted cheek and fingerbone

His dress undone, its facing torn—
want threads the needle's eye:

Slender strand, I
am no avail (cloud trail)

Any bolder wanter
brings a winter

Its coat between
my legs along

A certain Cretan shore—
lipsticked in Iraklion

A dolphin throne
a double ask for copper, glass

Side by side see Poseidon
(a him) temple whores

*

Lost boy, sit.
My lapping lap

Is pretty,
is mine to call

A sail
a glyph,

Is yours
to call a stone

iii.

The Everyday and Scientific Experiences of the Thing

Our special hatred of death need not render our fragility odious.
Why should we wish to become less mutable?

GALILEO, *Third Letter on Sunspots,* 1612

Bagging It

Well now, words on a paper bag, photos of another time, reasons to rise, shine.

The sun has come and with it a bird, a light on a stone. The sun bridges this side and that side and what's the next word? Write always *alone*.

She sent me "to hot to hoot" but its palindromic nature is awry, not imbued with the perfection the word mirror requires, the fires? in the mirror? inquires? who's the fairest—and also, whose.

Star bright, star light, I saw a star shoot tonight, how assassination bullets have wounded this word, a pauper now, bereft and orphany.

Odyssey: the no-sayer says Nausicaa is like a shoot of palm.

A well-traveled, seasoned, a marine (as in sea, not shooting) he.

Once a he. Now a she. There's a palindrome, a friend at high speeds, on the low road, through the foam of thalassa thalassa, the sea.

What happiness and a relief I once again seem (and once and again seem to me) to be me. Call it quits, call the girl call girl, call myself Me. *Dokei moi*, indeed.

Now I have to take this paper bag always to go with me and
be my friend in every need or however goes that Everyman's
Library motto creed . . .

First, how autobiographically historically authentically
if nostalgically, I go for a cup of green tea.

Orpheus Under The Table

i.   *High Tea*

On being served ephemera:
Spot more?
No thank you yes please.
        (sotto voce: Quickly)

ii. *More Singing Underneath*

The table is covered with paisleys embroidered
with tongues of flame that look like sperm.

What of it? Once I sat at a table where
somebody served me
a plate of sex. A nice one,
I tasted
good.

Mellifluous, apis, mine own honeybee,
will you ever taste me?
I have the sexual parts of plants.

You fatten your cells for a baby bee now
at the edge of the other sea.
Dance a bee dance

in mind how good I smell.
Still, my outcast state
flower's a forwarding address.

Don't you think I wear it well,
this red dress, past-tense, old girl

thing dilemma, this
The Paisley Question Mark
(a mystery by Agathon Christie).
At least I recollect to ask:
O Meno, what is virtue?
Are virtues then a swarm of bees?
Does the eye of the hive have a bee's-eye view?
Which is to say anything but blue—
and many.

Call virtue
beezantine pleasure
petal leisure
fetal embrasure.
Hoard of honey.
Skeins of smoke knit a thought
for a fontanel to cross.
Con a text, shreve a loss.
A-swim in sperm.
Sutra, a thread of cloth
a cloth of gold
fiery tongues
silver spoons
and tea grown cold.

That's the context but it's all wrong.
It's talk through my tablecloth hat
from my unattached head:
so far below the salt
I'm under the table.
Even the song
plays dead.

iii. *Time Trials*

The body is the best mystery.
It wasn't, then it begins;
it is, then it ends.

One moment, he is my dog then a car
and a perfectly dog-shaped nothing on the road.

When yellow leaves or none or few do hang
that is now.
This was, too.

Grow, Little (go worm)

A terracotta chicken with cut-away view
reveals its brood of cigarette butts.

How nicely those *t*'s go together, like teeth
in all of the mouths of all of the people
who smoked and planted—oh I get it—seeds,
cigarette butt seeds in ashtray earth . . .

So sperm (which has no identity according
to recently discovered and unattributed notes
in a notebook given me by Mr. Beloved Lover,
long longed for long ago and long gone (some people
stretch it out), whose seed we saved in the name
of a strange conservation of energy)

and the fowl herself the egg
(the o: biology as identity)—and the offspring?

The hen looks off to the mountain view:
redwood, madrone, the haunches of hills of gold
against the banks of ranges of varying hue
deep for the mountains, pale for the fog—

So what. On my desk full of leaves
I had just written on, an inch-worm offsprung,
twig-colored, stood and wavered around;
I gave it the leaf that said *now* to crawl on.

Our sibling, it shares our longing
that chicken eat us all.

A Closer Walk With Thee

"And he [sic] walks with me and he [sic] talks with me . . ."
traditional Christian hymn

There was a shining place far out to sea. Then it rained on it.

Then I remembered I forgot to take my thyroid pill. Little. Round. White.

Then the waitress brought my single scrambled egg. Hen. It was so tiny and round in the middle of a big white plate, I looked down and laughed. Then in the middle of the whole-wheat toast, one little feather curved, balanced like a boat.

Then the woman running by me in the red raincoat and red glasses bowed her head like horses do, and passes.

Then I tried on the white shirt I got in the gay thrift store during the flood while the water came up over the sidewalk. Wait while I go do it. The tag says Pin Point Oxford. Shall I do that, too?

Then I bought a black grosgrain ribbon and draped it around my neck. They should have let me be an altar boy when I wanted so I stole the beeswax candle stubs.

Then I took off my three shirts because I was hot from walking.

Then the sun came out over the ocean and dazzled my eyes where I sat writing shirtless.

Then I got cold.

Then there were the white flowers, scalloped with a hole in the middle, many and small on the rained-on asphalt and the little girl's tricycle under the flower trees by the dog leash and her standing in the rain saying Daddy.

Then there was the grandmother looking woman with the grandmother kind of accordion plastic rain hat on and smiling.

Then there was the fire truck.

Then there was the itchy sweater on the neck.

Then there was the Where did I get this belly?

Then I remembered I forgot to look at buttons.

Then I found another copy of *Things Invisible To See*.

Then I thought it said "eye grace" and I almost wrote eye grass and now I can't remember what it did say. What if we said eye grasses instead of eye lashes.

Then I said goodbye to Anu in the rain and worried I hadn't done something right, but what.

Now rays like God in the Bible storybook are pyramiding onto the ocean. Birds are flying in a circle, too.

Now a different now the white bark of the eucalyptus branches beautiful against the evening clouds with the waxing moon.

And all the times I am thinking of you.

Wood (First Daughter)

The bugs plug in. So do some frogs.
And we—of your hipbone, your shoulderbone, soon.
I would like to do it with you so the look of you is the breeze:
I would be content that we might procreate like trees.

Attendance

There are a million of them,
their name must be Legion.

Before I wrote this, I held out hand with pen in it
to view its missing hunk of skin.

Visit 20 years after to the old lover: meet the wife,
the dark-haired girls at dinner.

Before writing "before I wrote," observing
a Sunday's offering: he's and she's baby-toting.

Even the Desired One's schoolfriend arrives
with husband and new baby.

After he leaves, find the Viennese composer's said of me,
"What a shame she has no children."

What does he mean?

Often in the dawn [s]he reckoned them up.
No one was ever missing.

After Dinner Deserter

Such nice thunder
and the lightning's flickering tongue
like a snake's, quicker

than yours, its voice gone fretful on the phone,
then gone forever
but once it lapped our juices up just like a little napkin.

Roadside Redaction

I am become flimsy, Egypt, flimsy.
The *y* & the *p yclept*, embraced.
Maybe I meant they yealpt.
Meaning into the street:
Camino del Monte Sol.[1]
Manhasset.[2] Bigelow.[3]
Tarried there.
An I unmet yet
signatory.
On forms, neat
address, no
dress on
me, no
whore for
Where, no
more, no
sirree.

---

1. Santa Fe, NM 1980
2. Jackson, MS 1989
3. Cambridge, MA 1995

Première Leçon

What is the best way to get to the *Place de l'Etoile?*

with eyes closed
with hands up
with box seats

through a coat sleeve
through skin speak
through the mouth of March

in a teaspoon
in a tongue tip
in a Necco wafer

above fire dogs
between sand storms
along arch ways

beside sea weeds
beneath moth wings
a holy stammer

No, you have mistaken the way, go back, and take the first
street to the left.

It is called Bell View
It is called Uncle Sam
It is called Chops-a-lot
It is called *Cimetière Marin*
It is called Hamlet

It is called Piglet
It is called Endless Summer
It is called Edith Teeth
It is called Hurts Me Too
It is called Guaranteed
It is called Surinam
It is called No Dairy
It is called Pink Triangle
It is called Ten Thousandth Thing

I want a taxi at once.

Stop. Wait. Quickly, I am in a hurry.
The first stairs to the right.
The stairs at the end.
The stairs at the end,
there is a little leaf on them.
Curled. Hurry.

What is this building?
When is it open?
How much do I owe you?

Woe upon woe.

What numbers have you?

I have the mumber of mxxxxxxxx
I have the mumber of mxxxxxxxxxx
I have the mumber of mmmmmmmmmmmmm
I have the mumber of mm

I have none.

Take two numbers at the lamp post.

Star.
Star.

C'est complet.

I am much obliged to you.

The Path Leading From Little To Much

Moon swung bare through the cold sea;
over the arctic a star stared.

Third knowledge comes from third eye.

What thing caused our Henry's weeping?
Something rich and red inside.

Third knowledge, third eye.

Hamlet's birthday's late this year.
The candles on his cake are bare.
Their warm breath in colder air
spells out *Ophelia* and then spells *Where?*

Snow needles the night garden,
shines on a parapet, shrouds a shoe.

Clairvoyance, *clair de lune*—gone
and where? Fragrance of rotten leaves
from the walled garden hidden wherein
the unicorn lay his horned head
in the virgin's lap a thousand years
ago. The same star stares.

A fish leaps. A fig falls
from that same tree
whose roots entwine the snake whose tongue
first tasted then described the fruit,
bit the dark

place between
knower and
what's known.

(ah, to be as you are known)

A weeping fish beneath the moon
a cold spoon
again the shoe
the shoe

Dux And Comes: Saving The Appearances
And All Fall Down

[DUX: 2. Music. The scholastic name for the theme or subject of a fugue, the answer being called the COMES.]

The bottle-green sea-glass stands in its fastness, my own Stonehenge, dead center ring of red cylinder, red pedestal, red pencil sharpener, brand "Dux." Its brand of shadow, cast by lamp, bereft of planet's motive roulette, can tell me nothing of impasse, despite impassive face. However, by my nature I serve it as sun: I speak. My lips fixing stars in their spheres make a turning. Each work in turn supplants its precedent: the heaven is scarred with arcs of light. My face is barred by these meteors' shadows, by the tiny dolmen-gnomon's races across my dial face. This face tells times, tells all I am of flux. "I hope," I said.

The candle sprouts a sole gold leaf that's burning down its branch, its speech. (A torch! This way aphelion comes!) That shadow, if any, has fallen off the table, an equator, mercator, or a stripe for Ubi Leones where they've swallowed the sun, or a spear in a torch-light procession to the other hemisphere.

"Red," I said: I'd read the Irishman's poem and it knew what I knew. Who? Not comes, but ducks down by the river, as he tells it, then sad sex comes anyway. I just didn't in my life what he in his verse regrets doing in his. Last night I played Celtic lyrics for his friend, the one with whom I didn't. Oh ratio, oh proportion, is this all of perihelion? Will I meet this man who can tell me how to say Siobhan? No time to wait.

The Timex hurries its second hand. Its silent stick before silent sweep belies the circle I read but don't believe. Am I to believe all my words are, soundlessly, even now wheeling to welcome me by following me, turned hoopsnake in a field of Newtonian love? Yikes. Something tickèd this way comes.

Well, I know an epicycle when I hear one, boy: the Seiko alarm saved from the rich girl's garbage definitely ticks. It has no second hand but can ring if I make it. If I make it—it looks like I'm clocked in. If I couldn't see the nose on my face for a gnomon, I'd have what's in front of it telling time all over it: the leaves are falling and the ducks flying swing indisputable spokes all over the place. Heraclitus' river is moving my face.

Here comes one hell of a perihelion, Irishman, and I leave to you whether it has anything to do with fire-haired stars: what's still is so still it's in circles. Everything else is in flames.

Black Hat Drownded Piece

Shadrack: The missionaries come tomorrow.
    Wash your face. Keep the cat
    His tail out from under—of that
    What is the name?
    The curvded piece of wood,
    The ark in which the blame
    Rocked back and forth from *should*
    To *want* to *sorrow*.

Meshack: Every survivor is wise.
    Wisdom is pleasure
    Through a sieve of fire.
    It's what touch denies
    That burned what flew
    With the dove, its pyre.

Abednego: There's no way to unknow
    Except you watch Noah
    Like he was tv.
    No missionaries come tomorrow
    Except they come by me.
    Pass the marshmallows, please.

A Sign's A Sign

I. *Signs And Portents*

The pilgrim to Mont Saint-Michel
will come away with a cockle shell
and has for hundreds of years.
There are walls that work like shells held to ears:
hear through them oceans of infidels,
a tide that undoes reason and roads.
Finger the pewter pin on the pilgrim's pocket.
Hier ist kein Warum reads the docket:
the dragon unslain at every low tide.

II. *Home On The Range*

The obvious thing is the fire.
And the smoke alarm.
The snow plough growls.
The green needled trees
give little shrugs in the wind.
Their trunks take them in.

A bird too unimportant to see
stitches one refugee trunk to another.
Eyelashes like sutures from looking all day.
A tiny green filament floats like a future
in a vision of lamplight
and cozy decor.

The smoke burns my eyes.
The finch flies.

Speaking as one element to another,
let me say fire is the cruelest mouth.
It always turns its tenants out.

The Obvious Thing
is a world away. A world away
they are burning the walls of museum halls
raised to warm the cockles of civilized souls.
They are burning the walls (infidels) for fuel.
Here, there are blinks, shrugs, arguments
over dinners. In the end
(GE and Whirlpool snug in their beds,
sugarplum fairies blah blah in their heads),
some believe in their rocking chairs
this death a world away isn't theirs.

III.

A tree trunk's a coffin
and lack of one is one, too.
Bumper stickers on the old RV
hold you to your lack of place
like a promise made to glue.

A sign's a sign. Watch for ice
on bridge. Pilgrimage
is for the birds who
twice switched window seats with you.
And you? Hard to swallow
neither change in itinerary
nor in range: in the Bihac pocket
there's no spare change.

Homologum

Worried that wood would come of the would
you gave me an ontological fright.
It wasn't my fault that I didn't know
goodnight didn't mean goodnight.

Censer/Censure

These words left her.

Bitter scent, fortune, and somewhere still smokes,
leaving the waves of the grain of the wood
like sea spray. So I turn at last to you,
insomniac sea. Your mind is a Thing
sleepless and solemn as the wind's
adultery with you. Say

Have seen more beautiful
than necessity, even.
Have known the dream
of great stones.

Always the ulcer
in the wood's heart
a first fire finds out.
Is the forest better off
then drowned beneath the sea?

The wind belongs to the trees now.
All night, you know it. In the morning,
sea waves of smoke rock the cold night air.
Bitter sea, bless me, I suffer your faithfulness.

No Count: Master Of The Starry Wheels

What is truth, said Pilot, and would not stay for an answer.

Him, they call The Obscure.
His purlieu is that seashore where
your longest night is always longer still.
Him they call The Obscure, whose dwelling was the light.

His curse: Reverence to every river!
His prayer: May they capitalize on the sea's desire.
The terrestrial condition is miserable; my profits accrue
to indemnity tables set for the ghosts of the guests of my losses.

My account:

One evening while moving the moon's ladder on the water,
I came upon Pilot in a robe of white skin.
Master of numbers! I hailed him.
A trident tattooed on his chin

grinned as he grimaced.
Beneath the heaven's cruel silver
on which he counts no longer, his tarnished
piety my prerogative, he answered me with the sea's

interrogative:
a thousand and one,
a thousand and you?

Noon Of Green Water

Behold, thou hast been careful for us with all this care;
what is to be done for thee?

And this girl with the prayers:
Prophecies, prophecies.
She stands among the five trees
and all those things that bind her,
born and unborn, fall away.

Like ash in air, seagulls.
The sky errant above the sea.
Under its blankets, deep in its dream,
a starfish makes its way
to the beak that bears its destiny.

A young girl has given me this message.

Let us be bound by these
(I think she means the trees)
here at the edge of a just-born noon.
For it is better to be bound
than to be without a bound.

An impatience is upon the waters
for the last word from my lips.
Sea, wash your cheeks with salt
as you would your stones.
Bourne is a word like stone: few mean it.

In any case, its case is not the last.

Consider the stranger!
(I think she means me.)
Hers is the hungry hour and the blind hour.
In the blind hour, what does she see?

The sea still is still the sea;
sands speak to sands
in the phrases of the moon:
she is come, again and again.

She hath builded an enclosure made of wings.
She hath bound with a binding made of waters.
The tree releases a leaf and the leaf
is the letter that gives her lips their name.

You see she is cared for carefully.
You see in her a word unbound
and ever-binding still.
But still her soul is vexed in her:
this girl with the prayers sleeps.

Exponential Episcopy, If Not Episcopation[E]

1. Although an angel understands himself by his natural power[x]

2. Nothing can be sufficient cause of its own being[y]

3. Therefore have men given the incommunicable name to stones[z]

x: all the philosophers, whether Greek or Latin, recognize a divine ravishment in the investigation of the works of God;

y: for while it describes a fact, it reveals a mystery:

z: they could think of nothing nobler than their bodies.

Some Examples Of Relational Dynamics

The day could wheel
the sun spin overhead
over hill, under covenant
the look of constant arrive
with open hand
on brow the invitation
lo, always divined:
what
"we" could write

*

ink: alleluia, fluvium, sinners all again hymn round

room: to bloom the silence, to whet and hone the pen

think: teacup elbow, bony floor, shadow falling in the door

whom: dirty shirtcuffs of the moon, loner at the laundrymat

history: justice dressed up with only us to go:

   un: the grunt of love uncovers

   dos: shoulder credos, medicine dance

   three: sheets of foolscap (don't ask me why)

*

aluminum moon pale
silvered and scaled as fishes
encircles the water, waters the plants
skin of a mountain mind for knives
severs the stem so I can see: *divides*
is what makes fly

*

that the pleasure of the sacred wash over
you without demur the jubilation, piercing,
in the soul of the flesh an arrow of light
the feather of the jay
the fletcher of the grass

*

one plum stone plants
its sharp tip in my tongue
so chosen to transcribe root's speech
the scripture risen from the pit
written inscription
ideographic beginning of fruit
and desert kingdom
yet dead kings eat no plums
however hard
they piled up stones
lo, I am with you always:
what
"one is one and all alone" would write.

Notes

"Where There's A Will (Away)": "the walls do not fall"—H.D. "hair wants cutting"—*Alice in Wonderland*

"Being And Seeming, In Public": "a likeable young woman"—a quote from my rather brief letter of recommendation from the Writers Workshop

"Forms of A(d)Dress": "thinking on thinking"—Aristotle on the prime mover (which for many years I took to be desire). See also the objective genitive in Genesis; in the Hebrew, the verb and its result recognize one another: the earth grasses grasses.

"Primer": italicized excerpts from Stevens's "Idea of Order at Key West"

"Looks Are Everything": *o dokei moi*—Gr., it seems to me

"Noah Takes Five": "But O Father William . . ."—*Alice in Wonderland*

"The Model": quotes Donne's "Song"

"Self Portrait As Platter On Wall": "tough on words" from Laura Moriarty's blurb for *Homing Devices* (O Books, 1998). "Take my head, refreshing foundry"—corruption of Neil Young lyrics ("Comes a Time")

"The Shrimpy Girl Talk": "The Ballad Of Barding Gaol" is from my manuscript *Homeseeker's Paradise,* excerpted on the Poetry Society of America website.

"The Gift Of Time": Djerassi's Resident Artist Program motto

"Automat": *Why Pear?* (Em Press) is Denise Newman's chapbook; "is human what we really mean?" in "Os/Tensorium" is from her *Human Forest* (Apogee, 2000)

"Orpheus Under The Table": virtue and bees from Agathon's questions in Plato's *Meno*

"Wood (First Daughter)": quote from Sir Thomas Browne

"A Sign's A Sign": Hier ist kein Warum—Here there is no why

The Contemporary Poetry Series

EDITED BY PAUL ZIMMER

Dannie Abse, *One-Legged on Ice*
Susan Astor, *Dame*
Gerald Barrax, *An Audience of One*
Tony Connor, *New and Selected Poems*
Franz Douskey, *Rowing Across the Dark*
Lynn Emanuel, *Hotel Fiesta*
John Engels, *Vivaldi in Early Fall*
John Engels, *Weather-Fear: New and Selected Poems, 1958–1982*
Brendan Galvin, *Atlantic Flyway*
Brendan Galvin, *Winter Oysters*
Michael Heffernan, *The Cry of Oliver Hardy*
Michael Heffernan, *To the Wreakers of Havoc*
Conrad Hilberry, *The Moon Seen as a Slice of Pineapple*
X. J. Kennedy, *Cross Ties*
Caroline Knox, *The House Party*
Gary Margolis, *The Day We Still Stand Here*
Michael Pettit, *American Light*
Bin Ramke, *White Monkeys*
J. W. Rivers, *Proud and on My Feet*
Laurie Sheck, *Amaranth*
Myra Sklarew, *The Science of Goodbyes*
Marcia Southwick, *The Night Won't Save Anyone*
Mary Swander, *Succession*
Bruce Weigl, *The Monkey Wars*
Paul Zarzyski, *The Make-Up of Ice*

The Contemporary Poetry Series

EDITED BY BIN RAMKE

Mary Jo Bang, *The Downstream Extremity of the Isle of Swans*
J. T. Barbarese, *New Science*
J. T. Barbarese, *Under the Blue Moon*
Cal Bedient, *The Violence of the Morning*
Stephanie Brown, *Allegory of the Supermarket*
Scott Cairns, *Figures for the Ghost*
Scott Cairns, *The Translation of Babel*
Richard Chess, *Tekiah*
Richard Cole, *The Glass Children*
Martha Collins, *A History of a Small Life on a Windy Planet*
Martin Corless-Smith, *Of Piscator*
Christopher Davis, *The Patriot*
Juan Delgado, *Green Web*
Wayne Dodd, *Echoes of the Unspoken*
Wayne Dodd, *Sometimes Music Rises*
Joseph Duemer, *Customs*
Candice Favilla, *Cups*
Casey Finch, *Harming Others*
Norman Finkelstein, *Restless Messengers*
Dennis Finnell, *Belovèd Beast*
Dennis Finnell, *The Gauguin Answer Sheet*
Karen Fish, *The Cedar Canoe*
Albert Goldbarth, *Heaven and Earth: A Cosmology*
Pamela Gross, *Birds of the Night Sky/Stars of the Field*
Kathleen Halme, *Every Substance Clothed*
Jonathan Holden, *American Gothic*
Paul Hoover, *Viridian*
Austin Hummell, *The Fugitive Kind*
Claudia Keelan, *The Secularist*
Joanna Klink, *They Are Sleeping*
Maurice Kilwein Guevara, *Postmortem*
Caroline Knox, *To Newfoundland*
Steve Kronen, *Empirical Evidence*
Patrick Lawler, *A Drowning Man Is Never Tall Enough*
Sydney Lea, *No Sign*
Jeanne Lebow, *The Outlaw James Copeland and
    the Champion-Belted Empress*
Phillis Levin, *Temples and Fields*
Gary Margolis, *Falling Awake*